General editor: Graham Handley MA PhD

Brodie's Notes on Laurie Lee's
Cider with Rosie

Kenneth Hardacre MA
Formerly Head of English, Queens' School, Bushey

D1313273

Pan Books London and Sydney

This revised edition published 1986 by Pan Books Ltd
Cavaye Place, London SW10 9PG
9 8 7 6 5 4 3 2 1
© Kenneth Hardacre 1986
ISBN 0 330 50218 2
Extracts from Laurie Lee's *Cider with Rosie*
are reprinted by kind permission of
The Hogarth Press
© Laurie Lee
Photoset by Parker Typesetting Service, Leicester
Printed and bound in Great Britain by
Richard Clay (The Chaucer Press) Ltd, Bungay, Suffolk

Contents

Preface by the general editor   5

The author and his work   7

Literary terms used in this study aid   11

Laurie Lee's art in *Cider with Rosie*

Approach and structure   12

Setting   15

Themes   16

People   19

Style   26

Chapter summaries, critical comment, textual notes and revision questions   32

General questions   55

Further reading   58

For easy reference in these Notes the chapters of *Cider with Rosie* have been numbered 1–13.

Page references in these Notes are to the
Penguin edition of *Cider with Rosie*,
but references are also given to particular
chapters, so that the Notes may be used
with any edition of the novel.

Preface

The intention throughout this study aid is to stimulate and guide, to encourage the reader's *involvement* in the text, to develop disciplined critical responses and a sure understanding of the main details in the chosen text.

Brodie's Notes provide a summary of the plot of the play or novel followed by act, scene or chapter summaries each of which will have an accompanying critical commentary designed to underline the most important literary and factual details. Textual notes will be explanatory or critical (sometimes both), defining what is difficult or obscure on the one hand, or stressing points of character, style or plot on the other. Revision questions will be set on each act or group of chapters to test the student's careful application to the text of the prescribed book.

The second section of each of these study aids will consist of a critical examination of the author's art. This will cover such major elements as characterization, style, structure, setting, theme(s) or any other aspect of the book which the editor considers needs close study. The paramount aim is to send the student back to the text. Each study aid will include a series of general questions which require a detailed knowledge of the set book; the first of these questions will have notes by the editor of what *might* be included in a written answer. A short list of books considered useful as background reading for the student will be provided at the end.

Graham Handley

The author and his work

After reading *Cider with Rosie* the student will already know many of the facts of Laurie Lee's early life, for, although the story which this book tells is sometimes embellished and not always presented chronologically, its main outlines are very much those of reality.

We learn very little of Lee's father. A grocer's assistant with ambitions to enter the Civil Service, he had charm and talent. His first wife bore him eight children, of whom five survived, and when she died he advertised for a housekeeper for himself and four young children (his eldest child, Reggie, was living with his grandmother). His advertisement was answered by an attractive woman of thirty, Annie Light, the daughter of a Berkeley coachman. She had left school at thirteen to look after five younger brothers and had later gone into domestic service. She preserved a lively mind and an interest in music, poetry and painting, even when, returning from service, she helped her father run a village inn, doing most of the work herself and handling the drunks with firmness.

Annie and the young widower fell in love, married and lived in Stroud in Gloucestershire. They had four more children, of whom Laurie, born in 1914, was the youngest but one. When Laurie was three his father left home to join the Army Pay Corps and never returned, eventually joining the Civil Service and settling in London, where, thirty-five years later, he died. Annie and the eight children moved to a cottage in the village of Slad, near Stroud, and here Laurie was brought up. He was educated at the village school and later at Stroud Central School.

His formal education, he tells us, provided him with 'nothing more burdensome than a few mnemonics, a jumbled list of wars and a dreamy image of the world's geography'; but there were 'the less formal truths – the names of flowers, the habits of birds, the intimacy of objects in being set to draw them, the treacherous innocence of boys, the sly charm of girls, the idiot's soaring fancies, and the tongue-tied dunce's informed authority when it came to talking about stoats'. And – important for the future – young Laurie liked writing. No matter what the subject, his essays won approval and he could turn out a dozen poems an hour. It is clear that, from quite an early age, he came to regard the handling of words as the weaving of a net by which he tried to grasp those feelings and experiences which lurk just below the threshold of consciousness. He writes (in Chapter 9 of *Cider with Rosie*) of the 'stain of darkness' on his brow and the sinister door in his brain 'through which I am regularly visited by messengers whose words just escape me, by glimpses of worlds I can never quite grasp, by grief, exultation, and panic . . .' Later, in adolescence, he would sit on his bed and, staring out at the nibbling squirrels, make up poems. (Chapter 13).

On leaving school, at the age of fifteen, Laurie worked as a junior in an office in Stroud and in his spare time ran a local dance band. In 1935 he left home to seek his fortune. He walked to Southampton and then along the south coast to Worthing, earning enough money to pay for food and lodging by playing his violin. A month later he reached London, where he worked as a builder's labourer, took part in a strike, experienced a political awakening, 'the first sweet whiff of revolution', and won a poetry prize in a newspaper competition.

A year later he decided to go to Spain and landed at Vigo on the north-west coast with a knapsack containing a blanket and a spare shirt, a few shillings in his pocket and his fiddle, with which he proposed to support himself. The story of the next few months is told in *As I Walked Out One Midsummer Morning* (1969), another autobiographical volume, which provides a sequel to *Cider with Rosie*. Lee walked right across Spain, meeting people of all kinds and classes, sleeping in the open air and in squalid inns, playing his violin in streets, cafes and bars.

In Toledo he met the expatriate poet, Roy Campbell, and his family, with whom he stayed for a week. Campbell discussed contemporary writers and read his verse to him. 'Nothing,' said Lee, 'could have suited me better at that place and time of my life . . . What had I read till then? – cartloads of Augustan whimsy; this, I felt, was the stuff for me.'

Lee moved on to the south of Spain, where he worked as an odd-job man and musician in an hotel and made friends with the local radical leaders, who dreamt of revolution and a world without church or government or army. This was in 1936. It was a period of increasing tension. 'I was there,' Lee wrote in an earlier book on Spain, *A Rose for Winter* (1955), 'when General

Franco made his journey from Morocco and Civil War exploded along the coast.' The dreams and the hopes for a better world were swiftly doomed – 'Very soon the yellow snub-nosed tanks came clanking along the road from Malaga, Italian bombers swooped over the Sierras, German warships shelled from the sea. The town fell; and the firing-squads cut short the brave words of the committee.' Soon a British warship came to collect Lee and another English writer; but, back in England, with newspapers and further knowledge, Lee realized more fully the scale and implications of the Spanish War. Disentangling himself from a girl, he worked his way through France and, with the help of a small band of revolutionaries, crossed the Pyrenees into Spain again, to help the left-wing cause. Later he travelled in the eastern Mediterranean and worked in Greece and Cyprus.

During World War II Lee was Publications Editor at the Ministry of Information, himself writing an account of life in Britain during these days, *Land at War* (1945). He also worked with the GPO Film Unit and the Crown Film Unit, travelling to Cyprus and India. Some of his experiences are related in a book which he wrote with Ralph Keene, called *We Made a Film in Cyprus* (1947). After the war he was Caption-Writer-in-Chief for the Festival of Britain and was appointed Curator of Eccentricities at the Festival Exhibition; for this work he was awarded the MBE. Lee married in 1950 and in 1982 was made a Freeman of the City of London.

All this time he had continued to write verse – poems of love and war, many of them written in Spain; vivid evocations of places (see 'Port of Famagusta', 'Bombay Arrival', 'Stork in Jerez'); richly sensuous descriptions of natural beauty, of the countryside and its creatures (see 'Field of Autumn', 'Christmas Landscape', 'April Rise', 'Larch Trees', 'Apples', 'Cock-Pheasant'), and even of a London square transformed in imagination into an underwater scene in the last greenish light of a damp evening (see 'Sunken Evening'). Some of his poems are woven from nostalgic recollections of his Cotswold childhood – for example, 'Village of Winter Carols' and 'The Wild Trees.'

Lee's poems have been published in four volumes, which have won several literary awards: *The Sun My Monument* (1944), *The Bloom of Candles* (1947), *My Many-Coated Man* (1955) and *Selected Poems* (1983). *Cider with Rosie* was first published in 1959. It had taken two years to complete and was written three times. Lee has also written a radio play, *The Voyage of Magellan* (1948) and a long essay on the birth of his daughter, *The Firstborn* (1964). This is reprinted, together with a number of other essays written over several decades, in *I Can't Stay Long* (1975). This book has three sections: one contains 'certain abstract considerations of love and the senses' and another is devoted to a series of voyages. The seven essays in Part One are of considerable interest to readers of *Cider with Rosie,* for they comprise 'some early recollections of my country childhood and my departure from it', and in one essay Lee discusses the writing of autobiography. *Two Women* (1983) is a tribute to Lee's wife and daughter and is illustrated with a wealth of his own photographs, many of them in full colour.

Literary terms used in this study aid

Alliteration The recurrence of the same sound at the beginning of words which come in close succession. E.g. 'bussed and buttoned', 'puppyishly pretty'.

Hyperbole A figure of speech which uses deliberate and obvious exaggeration for effect only. E.g. 'One felt she could grow roses from a stick or chair-leg, so remarkable was this gift.'

Malapropism The use of a wrong word through confusion with another word of similar sound. E.g. 'ammonia' for 'pneumonia'.

Metaphor Whereas in a simile two things are compared, in a metaphor the name (or action or quality) of one is transferred to the other. E.g. 'He was a nourisher of quarrels, as men are of plants, growing them from nothing by the heat of belligerence and watering them daily with blood.'

Oxymoron This figure of speech brings together contradictory terms in order to give extra point or emphasis. E.g. 'icy hot'.

Simile A figure of speech in which, for emphasis or effect, two unlike things are compared, introduced by 'like' or 'as'. E.g. 'I tuned up like an ape threading needles', 'With his hawk-brown nose and whiskered arms he looked like a land-locked Viking.'

Laurie Lee's art in *Cider with Rosie*

Approach and structure

Cider with Rosie is perhaps best described as an imaginative auto-biography. It is not a factual account of the author's life, an account of events and incidents, arranged in sequence (with dates), beginning with the author's parents (or even grand-parents) and proceeding in an orderly fashion from his birth, through his infancy and childhood, his education and his mental and spiritual development, up to the time of writing or to any earlier point where the author finds it convenient to stop. Nor is Laurie Lee's book a work of purely imaginative literature, like a novel, where the author uses his creative powers to invent the incidents of his story and the characters which people it. It is a book which lies somewhere between autobiography and novel, and it belongs in the lower reaches of that class of which the supreme example in literature is probably James Joyce's *A Portrait of the Artist as a Young Man*.

Cider with Rosie is the story of a Gloucestershire childhood, but it presents Laurie's childhood as seen by the adult that Laurie became; the incidents are determined by adult selection, coloured by adult impressions, and presented with all the conscious (and sometimes even self-conscious) artistry of an adult professional writer, who can heighten and tone down, exaggerate or underplay, as he wishes. He is not on oath to tell us 'the truth, the whole truth and nothing but the truth'. The truth he is seeking is imaginative truth; what he is saying is not 'This is what happened', but rather 'This is how it felt'. That is why Lee's introductory note warns us that 'some of the facts may be distorted by time'. It is almost certainly true that some of them have been distorted, in recollection or by imagination or by the very form of their expression, for effect. In this respect *Cider with Rosie* has much in common with the impressions of his childhood written by Dylan Thomas in *A Portrait of the Artist as a Young Dog*. Neither of them is a piece of pure recollection; both are, to some extent, at the mercy of words; and in both, childhood is not so much reflected in a mirror as seen through a very special kind of lens.

In Lee's case, the effect of the lens is to give emphasis to the eccentric or the grotesque, to heighten the colours of the natural world and throw a hectic glow over everything, to see in familiar and everyday experience aspects of the strange and the sinister. Jones's goat was 'a beast of ancient dream' and 'old as a god'. The wood-knots in the bedroom ceiling 'ran like Negroes in the dusk of dawn' or became 'the alphabet of a macabre tongue'. The face of brother Tony 'had at times the radiance of a saint, at others the blank watchfulness of an insect'. In Granny Wallon's kitchen seasons fermented and summers were brought to the boil. Farmer Wells is 'dressed in dung'. In boyish games on summer nights the hunters pursued the hunted 'through all the world, through jungles, swamps and tundras, across pampas plains and steppes of wheat and plateaux of shooting stars'. In the protracted delusions and nightmares of sickness young Laurie 'lived ten generations and grew weak on my long careers' and the illnesses and diseases he suffered in childhood were 'enough to mop up an orphanage'.

Almost everything is larger than life because the author is attempting to see everything through the eye of childhood (even though the results are presented with all the linguistic resources of an adult). Laurie was 'born' at the moment when he was set down from the carrier's cart and temporarily abandoned where the grass towered tall above him and the frenzied larks screamed overhead. And when, just three feet high, he first goes to school, 'the playground roared like a rodeo'. After the Peace Day procession the squat and solid five-year-old finds himself in a strange world, where 'flags and roses moved against the sky, bright figures among the bushes'; and he sees around him 'a collection of upright tigers, a wounded soldier about my age, and a bride on the arm of a monkey'. For the adult author the light of imagination brings to his past the same kind of transformation as that which the swift arrival of winter brought to the young boy's familiar surroundings – 'The day came suddenly when all details were different and the village had to be rediscovered.'

Recollection and imagination do not easily allow themselves to be tied down to the rigid order of a time-sequence and it would be a mistake to expect that a book of this kind should have the structure of a novel. *Cider with Rosie* is a series of sketches of childhood and its environment and was developed out of 'fragments' which were originally magazine articles. They are of course woven into a certain unity through their common viewpoint and the fact that the central character grows up – the early chapters are concerned with infancy, the last two with puberty and adolescence; the descriptions of the cottage and of the author's brothers and sisters naturally come before those of school and classmates. But within this loose framework there is much fluidity. A full description of Laurie's Mother is delayed until Chapter 6 (she occupies the centre of his book, as she occupied the centre of his life); we learn little of his father until Chapter 4, and most of what we are told of him is in Chapter 7; we hear nothing of his sister Frances until more than half-way through the book.

Certain sections of *Cider with Rosie,* however, have their own pattern and structure. The first three chapters hang together: they present the child's gradually widening horizons, his explorations – the bedroom, the cottage, the garden, the fear-some figures of the 'world' beyond, and then school and class-mates, before returning to the central scene of activity, the kitchen. After this the framework is expanded and the story moves beyond the kitchen to the village and the valley. Looking back later on the composition of *Cider with Rosie,* Lee wrote: 'I became at this stage less a character than a presence, a listening shadow, a moving finger, recording the flavours of the days, the ghosts of neighbours, the bits of winter, gossip, death.' This is certainly true of Chapters 5–8 and Chapter 10 ('The Uncles'), but in the remaining chapters Laurie is very much the centre of the picture.

Chapters 5 and 6 stress the links between present and past – Laurie's childhood is set against the background of old people (Granny Trill, Granny Wallon, Mr and Mrs Davies, Joseph and Hannah Brown). The two parts of Chapter 8 ('Winter and Summer') are consciously balanced and each has a parallel pat-tern – impressions of early morning, the new world out of doors, the communal activities at night. The five-mile carol singing tour is balanced by the game of Fox and Hounds throughout the length of the same valley; Farmer Wells's calves by Mr Brown's horse; and Jones's pond is the central part of both sections. Chapters 11 and 12 return to the theme of widening horizons and the exploration of strange country – in one ('Outings and

Festivals') the explorations are largely geographical; in the other ('First Bite at the Apple') they are mainly sexual.

Setting

An important element in *Cider with Rosie* is the setting against which Laurie Lee's account of his childhood is presented – a detailed and clearly realized setting in place and time.

The cottage, once a small 17th-century country manor and later divided into three dwellings, is in Slad, a small village of twenty or thirty houses situated on the hillside of one of the five valleys which radiate from the town of Stroud, on the south-west edge of the Cotswolds in Gloucestershire. This particular valley, Lee tells us, was 'narrow, steep, and almost entirely cut off'. In the middle of the village was the Squire's Big House. 'Apart from the Manor, and the ample cottage gardens . . . all other needs were supplied by a church, a chapel, a vicarage, a manse, a wooden hut, a pub – and the village school.' Before the days of motor-cars and buses the only form of public transport was that provided by the carrier-carts which ran to Stroud. Otherwise, in days before the bicycle, if the villager without a horse went anywhere he went on foot, as did Laurie's family when they visited relations in Sheepscombe. People seldom strayed beyond the parish boundaries, except for the annual Choir Outings, at first by farm-wagon, later by horse-brake, and later still by 'the powerful new charabanc'. With the immediate vicinity of the village – the Catswood Larches, the Scrubs, Bulls Cross, Deadcombe Bottom, Brith Wood – Laurie and his friends were completely familiar. Villages like Painswick, Sheepscombe, Rendcombe, Bisley, Woodchester, Birdlip, Quedgeley and Churchdown, all of them within ten miles of Slad, seemed more remote; and places like Berkeley, Bristol, Gloucester ('once a foreign city') and Weston-super-Mare belonged to another world.

The time-setting of *Cider with Rosie* is roughly the second decade of the present century. (Laurie Lee was born in 1914; he left his second school in Stroud at the age of fifteen; and in 1935 he left the village of Slad for good.) It was the period of jazz-debs and the Savoy Orpheans, of wagonettes and unmetalled country roads, of *Home Notes* and the Home and Colonial stores, of the Tortoise stove and the Workhouse; when women wore beaded chokers and crochet-work gloves, and old ladies still dressed in poke bonnets, high-laced boots and black candlewick shawls.

In a period just prior to the development of so many of the drugs and medicines now available for the treatment of illness, sickness and infant mortality were depressingly common. 'Those were the days . . . when children faded quickly.'

Among Laurie's earliest recollections are the appearance of a soldier from World War I and the news that that war was over. He first remembers his uncles as 'khaki ghosts coming home on leave from the fighting', and the first big festival he can recall was the Peace Day celebration of 1919. By the late 1920s the village saw the coming of the motor-car, 'the clamorous chara-banc' and the solid-tyred bus, and soon found itself in a different age.

Themes

Life in an agricultural community is naturally closely bound up with the revolving cycle of the year, and the story of Laurie's childhood is told against the background of changing seasons (see Chapter 8) and successive feasts and festivals (see Chapter 11). 'From our seats in the choir,' he says, 'we watched the year turn: Christmas, Easter and Whitsun, Rogation Sunday and prayers for rain, the Church following the plough very close. Harvest Festival perhaps was the one we liked best, the one that came nearest home.'

Throughout the book the author reveals his vivid consciousness of time. In his earliest years 'time hung golden and suspended'; he cannot understand why autumn should not continue for ever, the end of the war must mean the end of the world. At the end of his story he realizes the 'the last days of my childhood were also the last days of the village'.

Cider with Rosie is a portrait of change; and that portrait is presented for the most part in human terms (infancy, youth, old age, death) through the various characters in its pages. In this respect the stories about the old people of the village (Mr and Mrs Davies, Joseph and Hannah Brown, for example, in Chapter 6) have a special importance. This portrait is also given depth by augmenting Laurie's own recollections with those of previous generations – his Mother's stories of her early days in domestic service and, further back still, Granny Trill's story of her father's death and her rescue by the Squire. The tree planted by Granny Trill's father is seen as a direct link with the distant past (see Chapter 5, p.87).

Similarly, the brooding superstitions and sinister legends, the memories of the older villagers, strengthen community-consciousness (Chapter 6, p.105).

In this context the episodes of the Bulls Cross Coach, Hangman's House, the murder of the returning emigrant and the suicide of Miss Flynn assume a greater importance than the furnishing of a few sensational stories: 'The village in fact was like a deep-running cave still linked to its antic past . . .' (Chapter 6, p.104).

In the days before television took up so much time, people talked more. Their homes were filled with *conversation* and children learned much simply by listening to this conversation. In this way young Laurie's horizons were widened by the stories told by his uncles – 'of campaigns on desert marches, of Kruger's cannon, and Flanders mud; of a world that still moved at the same pace as Caesar's' (Chapter 10).

Because of its isolation the village has its traditional patterns of security and social hierarchy. Its inhabitants had three ways of living. Most of them worked on the farms. Some worked in the cloth-mills, offices and shops of Stroud (Dorothy was a junior clerk, Marjorie worked in a milliner's store, Phyllis in a shoe shop). Others worked for the Squire. The latter was the apex of village society: 'The year revolved around the village, the festivals round the year, the church round the festivals, the Squire round the church, and the village round the Squire. The Squire was our centre, a crumbling moot tree.' When the Squire died the village community fell apart: the estate was broken up, the Big House was sold by auction and the servants went to work in factories.

The church was the other important element in the preservation of social stability, sense of community and class distinction in the village, before it too began to find its hold was weakening; and the scene in church on Sunday morning reflects the social pattern of the village (Chapter 13, p.219).

Cider with Rosie is as much the portrait of the village as of Laurie Lee himself, for he belongs, he says, to the generation which saw by chance the end of a thousand years' life, the end of the English village. Most noticeable, of course, were the physical signs. The horse gave way to the internal combustion engine. Instead of picnics and 'tribal wanderings' after nuts and blackberries, there were 'motor-bike jaunts and quick trips to Gloucester to gape at the jazzy shops'. The self-reliant activities round the kitchen table in an evening were replaced by the passive pleasures of the new picture-palaces. All these were at once the reflection and the cause of a change of spirit. The village began to look outwards: its values and its tastes were imported. The elemental bases of traditional village life, hard work, patience, closeness to nature and natural forces were shattered by speed, hysteria, 'fragmentation, free thought'; and pleasures, more 'tasty', were also 'more anonymous'. 'Soon,' writes Lee, 'the village would break, dissolve, and scatter, become no more than a place for pensioners.'

Two other themes are touched on more briefly and dealt with more concisely. The first is the content and aims of village education (nothing abstract, but simple patterns of facts and letters in Chapter 3 ('Village School'). The second is village morality – an acceptance of crime and misdemeanours as part of human nature, to be dealt with quickly and directly without the impersonal (and often demoralizing) processes of the law (see Chapter 6, 'Public Death, Private Murder', and Chapter 12, 'First Bite at the Apple').

People

The student might perhaps have expected this section to bear the heading 'Characters'; but to use that term here would be misleading, for *Cider with Rosie* is not a novel and the human figures which appear in its pages do not have the function of characters in a novel, invented to play a part in a sequence of events, initiating or being governed by those events and changing or developing in the course of them, thus contributing one of many elements to the total complex effect of the novel. In *Cider with Rosie* the human figures simply populate a landscape – either the Gloucestershire landscape of the setting or the imaginative landscape of Laurie's childhood. They are more like the figures in a painting, cleverly observed, skilfully drawn, perhaps caught in a characteristic attitude, but static for the most part, those in the foreground being larger and shown in more detail, those in the background or the less important corners being more shadowy and more lightly sketched in – head-and-shoulder portraits, as it were. In *Cider with Rosie* more than a hundred people appear, each with 'a local habitation and a name'. In some cases their part is limited to a single scene: they play that part and move off into the wings, giving place to others. Some of them have brief walking-on parts. Few of them appear in more than one scene.

Laurie

The central figure is of course that of the narrator-observer, Laurie himself. Suffering a whole succession of illnesses as an infant, he is haunted by 'the marching of monsters' (the result of early headaches) and a variety of night-time fears (see Chapter 2, 'First Names'). Though he is timid and fearful, he is also curious and eager to explore his surroundings. As he grows older, he grows tougher, turning his attention 'more towards the outside world, which by now was advancing visibly through the mist'. He soon grows used to the rough-and-tumble of school and taking part in all the tricks and truancy of his contemporaries. Plump in figure, he toughens up in the company of other boys; and though his childhood is still punctuated by returns of illness, he joins in all the boyish games – cricket, Fox and Hounds, ducking pigeons in a water-butt, sliding on the frozen pond, playing in the ruins of Hangman's House – and is always hungry. In evenings indoors he practises the violin and draws at the kitchen table. At school he develops a facility for handling words, can write long essays on the lives and habits of otters (though he had never seen an otter) and turn out poems by the dozen, with no effort. We learn more and more of what is happening *inside* the young Laurie. Long periods of solitary sickness foster his secret dream – his origins are mysterious; he is really a young king secretly placed among commoners, with a monarch's whims (like commanding a parade of grandmothers) and a concern for his anxious subjects (see Chapters 3, 'Village School'; 5, 'Grannies in the Wainscot'; and 9, 'Sick Boy'). From the beginning he had been haunted by 'the infinite possibilities of horror'; illness sharpened his awareness, so that his senses 'vibrated to every move of the world' and he was made one with the village in 'a kind of pantheist grandeur'; an accident caused a concussion which 'put a stain of darkness on my brow and opened a sinister door in my brain' (Chapter 9). The final picture is of the shifting balances of puberty and the first sexual urges (Chapter 12, 'First Bite at the Apple'), and the solitary dreaming of adolescence (Chapter 13, 'Last Days').

Laurie's family

After Laurie himself, the most detailed portrait is that of his *Mother*. The greater part of the material for this is to be found compactly presented in Chapter 7, which the student should consider carefully, together with the summary commentary of that chapter (p.41). This should, however, be augmented by those sections of *Cider with Rosie* which describe her activities on the first day in the cottage and on washdays (Chapter 1), the account of her sleeping and of her reactions to rain and flood (Chapter 2), her concern for Laurie in his sickness and her care of him during his convalescence (Chapter 9), her visits to relations, her unpunctuality (Chapter 11), the picnics she arranged and the quarrels with her daughters' fiancés (Chapter 13).

At school she wrote the best essays in the class; she loved reading and learning poetry by heart. As a young woman she was beautiful, mischievous and muddled-headed, with a stormy temper, a superior wit and considerable taste and sensitivity. In later life she played the piano, read Ruskin and Tennyson and the lives of the saints, was familiar with the work of Henry Tonks, and had a detailed knowledge of various kinds of porcelain and china, as well as the family trees of all the European Royal Houses. Though she spent some years in domestic service away from her native Gloucestershire, she was a country girl all her life and her portrait is a pattern of confusions (Chapter 7, p.133).

Soon after she learned of the death of her absent husband she too died.

Laurie's *Father* is a shadowy figure, for Laurie hardly knew him. He is described as 'a knowing, brisk, elusive man', 'much addicted to gloves, high collars, and courtly poses' (Chapter 4). His first wife had died while still quite young and he was left with five young children. He was a church organist and an expert photographer, and Annie Light was quite bowled over by 'this rather priggish young man, with his devout gentility, his airs and manners, his music and ambitions, his charms, bright talk, and undeniable good looks' (Chapter 7). Though he was only a grocer's assistant when they married, he studied each night and later, after war service in the Army Pay Corps, he entered the Civil Service, settled in London and never returned to his wife and the children of his two marriages.

Laurie had two half-brothers: *Reggie*, who lives with his grandmother and plays no part in *Cider with Rosie*, and *Harold*, 'handsome, bony, and secretive', who worked as a lathe-hand.

Laurie's three half-sisters are part of his very earliest recollections, 'brushing off terror with their broad scoldings and affection', going about their household tasks 'with their flying hair and billowing blouses', looking after the home when their Mother was away (Chapter 1); sending Laurie off to his first morning at school (Chapter 3); gossiping about boys round the kitchen table (Chapter 4); and dressing up to visit Granny Trill (Chapter 5).

Marjorie, the eldest, was a blonde, tall, dreamy and gentle. In the Peace Day pageant she was dressed as Elizabeth I. She worked in a milliner's shop and her suitor was Maurice, a builder of barges.

Dorothy was dark and active, full of curiosity and impudence, 'a wispy imp'. It was her boredom that saved the infant Laurie's life when Mrs Moore, who thought he was dead, was laying him out (Chapter 9, 'Sick Boy'). She was a junior clerk in a cloth mill and, dressed on Peace Day as 'Night', she was 'an apparition of unearthly beauty'. Her boyfriend was Leslie, the shy local scout-master.

Phyllis, the youngest, worked in a shoe shop. She was cool, quiet, fragile and solitary, and loved to put her young half-brothers to bed, singing them to sleep with hymns. She was Queen Elizabeth's lady-in-waiting and later she was courted by Harold, the bootmaker.

Of the children of the second marriage, the eldest was *Jack,* and Laurie's close companion in boyhood exploits. At school 'his flashes of brilliance kept him twinkling away like a pin-table'; at home he worked at sums and 'had developed a mealtime strategy which ensured that he ate for two' (Chapter 4, 'The Kitchen').

Next came *Frances,* beautiful and fragile, who died suddenly at the age of four (see Chapter 9). After Laurie, the youngest member of the family was Tony, 'a brooding imaginative solitary . . . the one true visionary amongst us', who was impervious to both learning and authority and who would sit at school all day picking holes in blotting paper (see Chapters 3 and 4).

Of Laurie's maternal grandfather, John Light, the Berkeley coachman who later became the landlord of the Plough Inn at Sheepscombe and spent most of his time playing the fiddle (did Laurie inherit his talent?), little need be said here (see the first two sections of Chapter 7, 'Mother'); nor of his five sons, who are given a portrait gallery to themselves in Chapter 10.

Other characters whose parts are confined to single scenes are: Granny Trill and Granny Wallon (Chapter 5), the eccentric Miss Flynn and those examples of marital devotion, Mr and Mrs Davies and Joseph and Hannah Brown (Chapter 6). Something has already been said of the gentry of the village (see p.17), chief among whom was Squire Jones, who appears briefly and inef-fectively on most of the village's important occasions, like the Peace Day celebration and the Parochial Church Tea. He looked after young Alice Trill on the death of her father; his 16th-century manor-house was always the first to be visited by the carol singers, who caught a glimpse of him standing on the stairs; his goat struck terror into the villagers and his pond was a focal point for the boys in winter and summer alike.

Another section of Lee's vast gallery contains the portraits of his school teachers: the beautiful and conforting sixteen-year-old junior teacher; the opulent widow with the hairnet which Laurie thought was a wig; the belligerent Miss B ('Crabby'), the sympathetic Miss Wardley, and Miss Bagnall, the Sunday School teacher who also held weekly dances.

Villagers, farmers etc.

It would seem that Laurie Lee can recall, at least by name, almost every one of the inhabitants of those twenty or thirty houses in the village of Slad, and some of them are associated with particular episodes in the book. Apart from those who have already been discussed or mentioned, these include the Bulls Cross hangman, the old soldier who was a deserter, Vincent from New Zealand and Fred Bates, the milkman, who came upon the drowned Miss Flynn, saw a man crushed to death by a wagon and was subsequently avoided as having inauspicious associations. There are others whose only part seems to be to help to give some general depth to the rural scene (Farmer Lusty, Farmer Wells, Farmer Joseph and Mr Brown, the builder) or to some aspect of village life, like the Parochial Entertainment (Major Doveton, Baroness von Hodenburg, Miss Pimbury and John Barraclough), or the church (Mr Crosby, the organist, Rex Brown, the organ blower, Widow White, who cleaned the church, and the vicar who confiscated *Sons and Lovers*). Then came those who are merely names, or little more – Jack Halliday, Miss Turk, Mrs Tully and Lily Nelson. The student should note, however, that even when Lee is introducing his minor figures he often identifies them with a sentence or phrase which serves as a label: Pug Sollars, Harry Lazbury and Mrs Moore, the Negress ('a jolly, eye-bulging, voodoo-like creature who took charge of us with primitive casualness'). The reader might sometimes feel that Lee loves a name, if only to conjure with, like that alliterative group of 'orbiting tramps', Harelip Harry, Davis the Drag and Fisty Fill; the other eccentrics who appear briefly in Chapter 2 illustrate his skill in providing a rapid thumb-nail sketch (see the paragraphs which he devotes to Cabbage-Stump Charlie, Albert the Devil, Percy-from-Painswick, Willy the Fish and Emmanuel Twinning).

Schoolmates

Much the same kind of comment and classification could be made of Laurie's contemporaries. Of some we learn very little – Clarry Hogg, for example, and Carry Burdock (sister of the immortal Rosie?); Jim Fern, slow of study and envious of Jack and Laurie; Clergy Green, 'the preaching maniac' (the phrase is never explained to us); Bill Shepherd, who first suggested the attack on Lizzie Berkeley and was himself later trapped by a girl; Walter Kerry, the bully whose yodel called the others out on summer nights and who later went to sea and won prizes for cookery. Some of these characters pop up from time to time in different parts of Lee's story. Such are the brothers Horace and Boney, who are always fighting others and usually coming off the worst for it in quarrels like those which arose during the carol-singers' tour as a result of Horace's breaking voice and Boney's insistence on singing a harmony to 'Noël'; later we are told of Boney's 'jackal scream' and how he was ultimately raped and married by a rich widow, 'who worked him to death in her bed and her barnyard'. Rosso the gipsy boy and Nick and Edna, who lived near Bulls Cross, are classed as 'outcasts' and described at the end of Chapter 3, and the Robinson children are described at the end of Chapter 8. Perhaps the best remembered, and certainly the most vividly presented, of all Laurie's schoolboy friends is Spadge Hopkins, who rebelled so spectacularly against 'Crabby' (Chapter 3, pp.50–51).

Of the girls a sharp impression remains with the reader, no doubt because they made a definite impression on Laurie himself. There was Vera, whose frizzy hair provoked him into hitting her on the head with a stick; Eileen Brown, with whom he played duets at the annual entertainment; Poppy Green, who, dressed as a spirit, finished the Peace Day celebration with torn wings and a broken lily; and Lizzie Berkeley blue-eyed, short and plump, who crayonned texts on the trunks of trees and somehow made the boys feel ashamed of their lustful fantasies. Finally we have a trio from whom young Laurie learnt much. Betty Gleed had eyes which were 'drowsy with insolence'; at eleven she was lusty, brazen and accommodating ('For a wine-gum she would have stripped in church'). Jo, with her 'cool face, tidily brushed-back hair, thin body, and speechless grace', became the map for Laurie's sexual explorations. Rosie Burdock, more devious, sly and provocative, has cat-like eyes and a curling mouth and on that afternoon she spent with Laurie beneath the hay wagon she was 'yellow and dusty with butter-cups and seemed to be purring in the gloom; her hair was rich as a wild bee's nest and her eyes were full of stings'.

Perhaps there are too many people in *Cider with Rosie*. They populate the landscape but they have no room to grow, to change, to develop. The reader does not know them long enough to gain more than an impression, striking and memor-able though that impression may sometimes be, or to penetrate beneath their external appearance. The description of Uncle Charlie, Aunty Fan and their children (Chapter 11) has warmth and understanding which are unspoilt by the search for the effective phrase, the comic touch, the distortion of the simple fact; and Laurie's Mother is presented with unsentimental ten-derness, with sympathy and with a depth that shows us aspects so different as to be almost different lives. But these are excep-tional. With most of his characters Lee's technique is that of quick and vivid recall – the technique of the snapshot – and the subject is highlighted with a striking phrase.

Style

There are two factors in the life and character of Laurie Lee that probably made it inevitable that he should become a poet and prose-writer. On the one hand is his heightened and vivid vision, his ability to experience the world around him on each occasion as if for the first time. Undoubtedly much of this was the result of a childhood punctuated by illness. When the fevers subsided, 'the real world seemed suddenly dear'; when sickness passed into convalescence his senses were 'tuned to such an excruciating awareness that they vibrated to every move of the world, to every shift and subsidence both outdoors and in, as though I were renewing my entire geography'. Lee himself says that an accident which caused concussion was also important (Chapter 9, p.168). On the other hand is his early facility for words and his delight in handling them, especially in the poems of his adolescence (see *The author and his work*, p.8); and this gift enabled him to translate the heightened vision into words.

Lee has said that *Cider with Rosie* is 'a celebration of living and an attempt to hoard its sensations' and that in writing it he was moved by the need 'to praise the life I'd had and so preserve it, and to live again both the good and the bad'. Throughout *Cider with Rosie* he makes the reader conscious of the utter profusion of experience, the variousness of the world, its abundant energy and its sensuous impact. As a result, he often pours out impressions in sentences which are little more than lists. One of his earliest memories is of crawling about on the floor of the kitchen among ornaments which had only just been deposited from the carrier's cart (Chapter 1, p.10).

Later the house is full of

an infinite range of objects and ornaments that folded, fastened, creaked and sighed, opened and shut, tinkled and sang, pinched, scratched, cut, burned, spun, toppled, or fell to pieces (Chapter 2).

The energy and activity of small children at tea-time is similarly conveyed by a succession of verbs (Chapter 4, p.72); and the same technique is used to describe the terrifying methods of 'Crabby' (Chapter 3, p.49).

Lee sometimes obtains the same effect of the breadth of life (and in this case of the expansion of the spirit) by the use of long, rolling sentences:

Until then we had chased them through all the world, through jungles, swamps, and tundras, across pampas plains and steppes of wheat and plateaux of shooting stars, while hares made love in the silver grasses, and the large hot moon climbed over us, raising tides in my head of night and summer that move there even yet (Chapter 8, p.154).

A similar sparkling vitality and the deft manipulation of words enables him to sketch a character in a few lines, especially if that character is unusual or larger than life. Consider Cabbage-Stump Charlie and Albert the Devil in Chapter 2 ('First Names'), the description of Spadge Hopkins in Chapter 3 ('Village School') and that of Uncle Ray in Chapter 10 ('The Uncles'). On other occasions Lee's quick character sketches and personal descriptions have the quality of almost physical richness e.g. the description of Poppy Green in Chapter 11 (p.184); or mysterious tenderness e.g. the description of Jo in Chapter 12 (p.204).

The same skill with words with which Lee describes people is shown in his ability to recreate physical and sensuous experiences, as in the paragraphs on water and on food in Chapter 1, and to evoke an atmosphere, as in his recollection of the hymn his Mother sang on the way to Sheepscombe (Chapter 11, p.189). Lee's narrative style is as varied as his descriptive prose. The student should compare his presentation of the swift and whirling panic of the incident of the flood in Chapter 2 ('First Names') and the deliberately melodramatic style of the story of the murder of Vincent in Chapter 6 ('Public Death, Private Murder') with the movingly simple, undecorated account of Mr and Mrs Davies later in the same chapter. The same variety is revealed by contrasting the solitary experiences of convalescence in Chapter 9 ('Sick Boy') and adolescent wandering in Chapter 13 ('Last Days') with the crowded scenes and activities of the occasions dealt with in Chapter 11 ('Outings and Festivals').

Cider with Rosie is also notable for its direct presentation of human life in talk and conversation (much of it tinged with the country flavour of dialect). Most readers will carry in their memories the clipped and crusty talk of Granny Trill (Chapter 5), the sullen argument between Jack and Laurie about the name of the king (Chapter 4), the impassioned quarrel when one of the sisters wants to leave home to be married (Chapter 13), the teasing from Uncle Ray (Chapter 10), the village women's chatter about Miss Flynn (Chapter 6), the boys' furtive conversation when they plan the 'Brith Wood rape' (Chapter 12) and the interwoven, disconnected observations of the different members of the family gathered round the kitchen table in the evening.

Three elements are more important than any others in determining the special qualities of Lee's style and all three are usually more closely associated with a poet than a prose-writer.

Simile and metaphor

Much of Lee's verse is notable for its unusual and striking imagery and the same skilful use of simile and metaphor is evident throughout *Cider with Rosie*. Some readers might think it is *too* evident and that imagery is almost an addiction or a device which Lee sometimes practises too consciously and deliberately; and certainly it is an element that he seems to have toned down in his later prose. But it is a characteristic feature of *Cider with Rosie*.

Eileen Brown's face, as she sits at the piano, was 'as white as a minim'. The pier at Weston-super-Mare was 'like a sleeping dragon'. When Laurie opened a calf's mouth it was 'like a hot wet orchid'. His mother was 'muddled and mischievous as a chimney-jackdaw'. His brother Tony's 'curious, crooked, suffering face had at times the radiance of a saint, at others the blank watchfulness of an insect'. Joseph and Hannah Brown 'resembled tawny insects, slow but deft in their movements; a little foraging, some frugal feeding, then any amount of stillness. As Laurie and his brother and sisters go to their beds in the 'patched and parcelled' cottage, 'each night was a procession of pallid ghosts, sleepily seeking their beds, till the candle-snuffed darkness laid us out in rows, filed away in our allotted sheets, while snores and whistles shook the old house like a roundabout getting up steam' (Chapter 4); and during Laurie's nights of illness 'the flame of the candle threw shadows like cloaks which made everything vanish in turn, or it drew itself up like an ivory saint, or giggled and collapsed in a ball' (Chapter 9).

Often the similes add a dimension of time that links the present with the remote past. The village of Painswick, seen from the hills, 'sprawls white in the other valley, like the skeleton of a foundered mammoth'; and to the eyes of young Laurie his uncles, 'bards and oracles each', seemed like 'a ring of squat megaliths on some local hill, bruised by weather and scarred with old glories'. Sometimes a number of similes follow each other in quick succession: e.g. Chapter 3, p.42.

The same kind of brilliance is provided in Lee's metaphors. Often they are brief and enlightening. While the family was moving into the cottage, the infant Laurie sat on the floor 'on a raft of muddles'. When he is seriously ill he sees around his bed 'a shroud of sisters'. The life of the village revolves around the Squire, 'a crumbling moot tree'. Lying on his back in summer fields, Laurie sees 'the grass scaffolding the sky' and 'cuckoos crossed distances on chains of cries'. Seen at night, Painswick was 'a starfish of light dilating in a pool of distance'.

Sometimes Lee carries metaphor almost to the point of hyperbole. The pier with its lurid peep-shows is 'a festive charnel house'. The buses which Uncle Sid drove are 'staggering siege-towers which often ran wild'. His uncles, on leave from the war, are 'riders of hell and apocalypse, each one half-man, half-horse'. At other times his metaphors suggest a secret delicacy, as when he says of Jo:

She became the pathfinder, the slender taper I carried to the grottoes in whose shadows I now found myself wandering (Chapter 12).

Occasionally he will develop a single metaphorical idea through a number of related phrases, e.g. the death of Granny Trill (Chapter 5, p.92).

Another example is the infant Laurie's impression of the scullery (Chapter 1, p.14). Best of all, perhaps, the description of Uncle Charlie's special gift (Chapter 10, pp.171–2).

Alliteration

A writer who handles words imaginatively is always conscious of the sound-patterns of his phrases and the reader should train his inner ear to become sensitive to these. Sometimes they may be simple repetitions of the same sound ('leafy levitation', 'crystal kingdom', 'freaks of frost', 'a morning of cows and cockerels'). More often they will combine more than one sound:

Meanwhile, reeking with power and white in the moon, he went his awesome way (m and w) (Chapter 2).

It towered above me and all round me, each blade tattooed with tiger-skins of sunlight (t, s and l) (Chapter 1);

or emphasize a metaphor to produce a greater depth of effect:

Proud in the night the beast passed by, head crowned by royal horns, his milky eyes split by strokes of midnight (Chapter2).

The thumping of heart-beats which I heard in my head was no longer the unique ticking of a private clock but the marching of monsters coming in from outside (Chapter 2).

Alliteration in Lee's prose is hardly ever onomatopoeic (sounds being specially chosen to echo the meaning of the subject-matter); it is simply the thread which stitches more closely together the parts of a phrase or sentence. If the student now re-reads the examples quoted in the sections above on simile and metaphor he will find many alliterative effects there also.

Rhythm

Lee is a writer whose choice of words and pattern of sentences is much influenced, and sometimes dictated, by his sense of rhythm; and since he is also a poet this is not surprising. It is a feature that is most noticeable in his cadences, that is, the rhythmical flow of words, especially at the end of a sentence. Lee has a particular fondness for arrangements of anapaest (xx′) and iamb (x′) and sometimes these are so insistent that one has the feeling that one is reading verse, not prose.

It smelt of ripe grass in some far-away field and its taste was as delicate as air (Chapter 5).

Her hair was as rich as a wild bee's nest and her eyes were full of stings (Chapter 12).

If the student cultivates his sensitivity to these rhythms he will become aware that Lee has a special liking for three patterns of sentence-ending, which occur again and again.

(i) xx′/x′/xx′

The old men listened, and the young men watched,
with the oil lamps red in their eyes (Chapter 6).

(ii) xx′/xx′/x′

. . . revealing our faces more by casts of darkness
than by any clear light they threw (Chapter 4).

(iii) x′/xx′/xx′

. . . stranger than flesh, smoother than candle-skins,
like something thrown down from the moon (Chapter 12).

Once he is alerted to Lee's rhythms, the student will find scores of examples of these three patterns. They are an importat ingredient in the particular flavour of his prose style.

Chapter summaries, critical comment, textual notes and revision questions

Chapter 1: First Light

The author recalls his earliest memories. For him life seemed to begin when his family moved to the village in 1918. He remembers being lost and the comfort of his sisters, the chaos of the first day in the cottage, his growth, his early fears, his impressions of the cottage and his gradual exploration of its immediate surroundings, his 'discovery' of water, his enjoyment of food, his needless panic when he was unable to open his eyes one morning and his uncomprehending reaction to the approach of autumn. He describes a visit from a mysterious soldier. Laurie's mother goes away on a visit to the husband who had deserted her, leaving the girls in charge of the cottage. While she is away the village hears that the war is over. Laurie remembers the celebrations and how the schoolhouse chimney caught on fire.

Commentary

Lee plunges immediately into a vividly recalled physical experience: being set down at the age of three among tall grasses. This he describes with striking references to the senses of sight, sound (the chirping of grasshoppers and the screaming of larks), smell (the rank odour of nettles and the sweet fumes of elder-blossom) and the sensation of tropical heat.

All this helps to convey the *child's* sense of loneliness and bewilderment, but it is done through the *adult* writer's skill, with similes and metaphors in almost every line and much alliteration.

This initial picture is then 'framed', as it were, by the commentary of the adult looking back on the experience, in the paragraph beginning 'That was the day we came to the village' and the paragraphs that follow. In this way, here and throughout the book, the author makes use of a double sense of time – the child's present and the author's past.

An almost overpowering richness of language conveys the wealth of new experiences and impressions that crowd upon the young Laurie and in more complex areas, later in the chapter, we find a similar method: a very adult use of language brings us a child's gradual awareness of death (see p.14).

The special qualities of *Cider with Rosie* and some important characteristics of Lee as a writer thus become evident at the outset.

Later in the chapter come the first hints for the young Laurie of a world beyond the cottage and his own family. The appearance of the soldier, who, though Laurie doesn't realize it at the time, is a deserter from the army, leads to some very vague ideas about the war. (Later he will learn more about soldiers from Uncle Charlie and Uncle Sid – see Chapter 10). The villagers' immediate and spontaneous celebration of the end of the war fills his mind with unanswerable questions, especially about his father, who had left the family and, apart from the occasional visit, had never returned. (The official celebration in the village, Peace Day in 1919, is one of the festivals described in Chapter 11).

the age of three Laurie Lee was born in 1914.
village Slad, two miles north-east of Stroud, in Gloucestershire.
syringa The mock-orange, a sweet-scented white shrub.
half-remembered landscape i.e. his previous home.
time hung golden and suspended A phrase reminiscent of the Welsh poet, Dylan Thomas (1914–53). Cf. his poem, *Fern Hill*.
bussed Kissed.
Bubble . . . grumble An adaptation of the chorus of the witches' song in Shakespeare's *Macbeth*:

Double, double, toil and trouble,
Fire burn and cauldron bubble.

hunger of eight i.e. Laurie, his Mother, his brothers Jack and Tony, his half-brother Harold and his half-sisters Marjorie, Dorothy and Phyllis.
bush of Moses When God's call came to Moses it was accompanied by the appearance of a burning bush which was not consumed. See Exodus, 3,2.
Loll The family's pet name for Laurie.
brassoed With polished buttons, buckles etc. Brasso is the proprietary name of a make of metal polish.
sodger The Gloucestershire pronunciation of 'soldier'.
Thee s'll Country dialect for 'you will'.
our father Further information about Laurie's father is to be found in Chapters 4 and 7.
Kaiser William II, Emperor of Germany and King of Prussia at the time of World War I. He was compelled to abdicate in 1918. 'Kaiser' is the German equivalent for Emperor (cf. Latin *Caesar*, Russian *Czar*).

Chapter 2: First Names

The coming of peace makes no appreciable difference to the quality of the infant Laurie's life. He no longer shares his Mother's bed and he is haunted by a daylight uneasiness and various night-time fears. He recalls a frightening visit from Jones's goat, describes other terrors, including a Two-Headed Sheep and the Bulls Cross Coach, and tells the story of Hangman's House, where he and his brothers played. There follow descriptions of eccentric neighbours – Cabbage-Stump Charlie, Albert the Devil, Percy-from-Painswick, Willy the Fish, John-Jack and Emmanuel Twinning. The chapter ends with a description of the drought of 1921 and the effect of the subsequent rain and floods on life in the cottage.

Commentary

A useful key to the four sections of this chapter is the phrase 'my first dose of ageing hardness', for after having to leave sharing his Mother's bed and never being allowed to return, Laurie turns his attention more to the outside world. Its first impact is 'through magic and fear'; then come descriptions of some alarming village characters and finally the panic accompanying the flood which follows the great drought.

sloes The fruit of the blackthorn.
blind bare arms The adjective 'blind' suggests restless, involuntary movement during sleep.
surrogates Substitutes. In the language of psychology a surrogate is a dream-figure used to conceal the identity of some other person.
lust In literature the goat is often associated with lasciviousness.
sheep-lightning This may be a local variant of 'sheet-lightning'.
Berkeley A small town near the mouth of the river Severn in Gloucestershire, some ten miles south-west of Stroud. See the opening paragraph of Chapter 7.
Birdlip A villiage on the edge of the Cotswolds, between Stroud and Cheltenham and six miles north of Slad.
Bisley A village two miles south-east of Slad.
Gloucester-Market The county town is eight miles north of Slad.
sin i.e. seen.
Painswick A small town in the hills, less than two miles from Slad.
Post Mail-coach.
tundra Treeless area; strictly, the name given to the flat, treeless regions with arctic climate and vegetation in northern Europe and Alaska.

soft-boiled eyes i.e. having something of the appearance of a soft-boiled egg.

orbiting i.e. travelling regularly round the countryside.

manic Suffering from a mental disorder.

familiars Close friends; originally, attendant demons.

Wales The border of Wales is some forty miles west of Slad.

skewbald A horse with irregular markings in two or three colours (usually white, brown and red).

O come, O come . . . The lines quoted here are the opening of a hymn, translated from Latin, by J. M. Neale (1818–66), a prolific writer of hymns who also wrote the carol, 'Good King Wenceslas' (see p.44).

murdering sleep Cf. Shakespeare's *Macbeth*, II,2, 36–7:

Methought I heard a voice cry, 'Sleep no more!
Macbeth does murder sleep.'

subpoenaed Literally, served with a writ from a court of justice which commands the presence of a witness under penalty for failure.

apostrophes A technical term in rhetoric for exclamatory addresses to some person or thing, present or absent.

bell-essed i.e. blessed.

Chapter 3: Village School

We are told of the influence of its geographical isolation on the life of the village and the kind of education provided by the village school. The author recalls his first day in the Infants room, his teacher and his companions (Poppy, Jo, Vera and his brother Jack). When he moves to the Big Room he is taught by Miss B ('Crabby'), the Head Teacher against whom Spadge Hopkins one day rebels, and her successor, Miss Wardley. It is at this period of his life that Laurie begins to enjoy writing. After summing up what he learned at school of 'the less formal truths' and personal relationships, he recalls the outcasts, Nick and Edna, and the gipsy boy Rosso.

Commentary

Lee concentrates on the characters and incidents of his school-days rather than the content and quality of the education it provided. Though he says he was content to bide his time, to loll around idly, it is clear that he was an apt pupil and left the Infants group with a good grasp of letters and numbers. In the 'Big Room' he learnt much more and began to develop and exercise his gift for writing essays and poetry, drawing on an unusually fertile imagination (writing at length, for instance, on the lives and habits of otters, though he had never seen an otter).

We are now introduced to a number of Laurie's contemporaries. Of most of them, apart from Spadge Hopkins, we learn little more than their names as yet, but we are to meet many of them again in Chapter 8 ('Winter and Summer') and Chapter 12 ('First Bite at the Apple').

The student should be prepared to differentiate Laurie's four teachers – the beautiful junior teacher who taught him to use a counting frame; the opulent widow whose hair net he mistook for a wig; the Head Teacher, Miss B ('Crabby'), who pounced without warning and aroused the displeasure of Spadge Hopkins; and Miss Wardley, who did not at first much approve of Laurie but liked his essays and won his respect.

Windrush The river Windrush rises in hilly country some twenty miles north-east of Slad.

Escarpment The steep slopes of the Stroudwater Hills.

some time before A deliberate understatement of course. The end of the Great Ice Age was about 20,000 years ago!

Roman snails After the common garden snail, the best known is the Roman snail, an edible variety which, in France, is cultivated as a food.

pre-Raphaelite goitres Reacting against the mid 19th-century fondness for the later Italian artists, a group of English painters, under the leadership of Rossetti, Holman Hunt and Millais, founded the Pre-Raphaelite Brotherhood, basing their principles of art on those of the early Italian painters.

Goitre is a disease which causes an enlargement of the thyroid gland of the neck. It is certainly true that large and prominent necks feature in many Pre-Raphaelite paintings of women (e.g. Rossetti's 'Beata Beatrix', 'Monna Vanna' and 'Proserpine').

Cotswold The Cotswolds is the name given to an area of Gloucestershire traversed by a range of hills running from north to south for more than fifty miles. The stone quarried from these hills and used for almost all the local building is of a warm golden-grey colour. Slad is on the south-west edge of the Cotswolds. The famous Cotswold sheep, with their long coats, have made the Cotswolds an important wool-producing area throughout history.

Stroud This Cotswold town, two miles from Slad, is the centre of the West of England cloth trade.

Universal education The basis of free and universal education in Britain was the Education Act of 1870.

rodeo Public display of cowboys' skill in horsemanship and the rounding-up of cattle.

Poppy Poppy Green appears again in Chapter 9.

Jo See Chapter 12.

You're 'alf . . . The more usual colloquialism is 'You are *not* half . . .'

pinafore In Lee's childhood it was customary for schoolchildren, boys as well as girls, to wear in school a covering of washable material to protect their clothes from being soiled.

Crabby From 'crabbed' – sour-tempered, ill-natured.

sharp nudge in the solar plexus i.e. a painful reminder that they were cut off from physical and sensuous enjoyment. The solar plexus is a network of nerves situated at the pit of the stomach.

leafy levitation Leaves floating in the air.

pin-table In one kind of pin-table the small metal ball causes electric bulbs to flash as it makes contact with the pins.

gurt i.e. great.

Chapter 4: The Kitchen

This chapter returns to the house and the life in it. After the departure of his father Laurie grew up in a world of women – his Mother and his three half-sisters, Marjorie, Dorothy and Phyllis. His two half-brothers stood somewhat apart; there were also his true brothers, Jack and Tony. The cottage is described: attic, bedroom and kitchen – the last being the place where most of their waking life was spent. The remainder of the chapter traces the course of a normal day – breakfast, play and dinner; the return to the kitchen in the evening and the lighting of the candles and the lamp. Laurie practises the violin while his Mother cooks pancakes and struggles with the fire. After tea the boys draw and play at the table, joined by Mother and the girls (each with her own task) and in the general conversation Laurie grows sleepier and sleepier.

Commentary

Laurie's Mother is given a chapter to herself later (Chapter 7). The portraits of his father and his half-sisters, and the briefer ones of his brothers and half-brothers, are some of the most impressive in the whole book. They repay careful reading and analysis. The student should note how striking (and sometimes unexpected) adjectives and similes – Dorothy is 'pretty and perilous as a firework', while Phyllis is 'a tobacco-haired, fragile girl, who carried her good looks with an air of apology' – effectively distinguish the characters of the girls.

The chapter summary above brings out Lee's skill in

organizing so much varied material around the threefold framework of people, place and time.

Aphrodite The name of the Greek goddess of beauty and love (the Roman Venus).
ratted Betrayed, deserted.
slack Composed of dust or very small fragments.
Stroud's five valleys These are clearly discernible on a relief map. The roads in these valleys lead from Stroud to Slad and Painswick, Cirencester, Nailsworth, Stonehouse, and Gloucester, respectively.
quartern loaves Made of a quarter (four pounds) of flour.
'William Tell' The overture to the opera 'William Tell' by Rossini (1792–1868) has always been popular in many different musical arrangements.
thou' Thousandth of an inch.
Beefeater The Warders of the Tower of London still wear the Tudor period costume of the Yeoman of the guard.
chicken-gah Chicken-dung (a country expression).

Revision questions on Chapters 1–4

1 Describe the scullery of the cottage and some of the activities that went on there.

2 What were the reactions of the family towards Jones's goat? Why did they feel this way?

3 What did Laurie and his sisters do when they heard that World War I was over?

4 Describe three of Laurie's eccentric neighbours.

5 Describe Laurie's experiences in the Infants Room.

6 In your own words, write an account of the rebellion of Spadge Hopkins against 'Crabby'.

7 What did the various members of the family do in the kitchen in the evenings?

Chapter 5: Grannies in the Wainscot

The house, once a small country manor, was divided into three cottages. In the other two lived two old ladies. Granny Wallon's chief occupation was making wines. Grany Trill, a simple, frugal creature, combs her hair, reads Old Moore's Almanac and tells the children of the death of her father, a woodcutter, and how she was then cared for by Squire Jones until her marriage. These two elderly ladies dressed for the part and Granny Trill took snuff. One day the girls dress up and visit Granny Trill, who is shocked by their airs and graces. The two old ladies were lifelong enemies until Granny Trill broke her hip in a fall and died. At the funeral Granny Wallon made a passionate outburst about Granny Trill's age, but soon afterwards she too faded and died.

Commentary

These two old ladies are among the most colourful in Lee's whole gallery, but they also have a special significance as 'death-less crones of an eternal mythology'. Granny Wallon, making her wines from almost every kind of flower and berry she can find, is a link with nature and the countryside. She is like some ancient fertility goddess, whose rites are attended by tipsy celebrants.

Granny Trill, a woodland creature, is also a direct link with the past of the village (see p.17). She is like some rural sibyl, with her eccentric sense of time and her preoccupation with prophecies of crises and catastrophes, and her stories of her father's death and the tree he planted extend the time-scale of Laurie's background into a past so distant that it seems to him the beginning of the world.

airy nothing . . . name Cf. Shakespeare's *A Midsummer Night's Dream*, V,1, 14–17:

> As imagination bodies forth
> The forms of things unknown, the poet's pen
> Turns them to shapes, and gives to airy nothing
> A local habitation and a name.

vestigial Surviving only as an imperfect form of an earlier, more primitive state or condition.

varmints Mischievous or troublesome children. (*Varmint* is a variant of *vermin*.)

almanac Originally an almanac was a book of tables of sunrise, sunset, changes of the moon, etc., with a calendar of church anniversaries and forecasts of weather. The original 'Old Moore' was a physician and astrologer called Frances Moore (1657–1715) who published an almanac to promote the sale of his pills. In more recent times there have been many versions of 'Old Moore's Almanac', containing so-called predictions of the sensational kind mentioned by Lee.

Antipoods i.e. Antipodes.

Crevice i.e. crevasse.

Scrubs A tract of countryside overgrown with brushwood and stunted trees.

poke bonnets Bonnets with projecting brims.

talked careful The phrase is itself an indiction that the sisters' attempts at correct English were not always successful.

jazz-debs Debutantes of the 1920s.

Home Notes A women's weekly paper of long standing, devoted for the most part to cookery and dressmaking.

baggages Pert and artful young women.

strictures Contractions of a duct or passage of the body, especially of the intestines.

steel-sprung boots Boots strengthened with a strip of steel.

Chapter 6: Public Death, Private Murder

This chapter recounts the murder one Christmas of a villager called Vincent, who returns, rich and successful, from New Zealand; the suicide of the eccentric Miss Flynn; the death of Mr Davies; and the lives and deaths of Joseph and Hannah Brown.

Commentary

The previous chapter concluded with the deaths of Granny Trill and Granny Wallon, and death, a frank and unfearful attitude to it and 'an acceptance of violence as a kind of ritual' are also the subjects of this chapter. But here they are part of a wider theme: they form one strand in a continuous thread that led backwards to the village's 'ghostly beginnings', 'the blood and beliefs of generations' which were often associated in a strange way with particular spots in the valley, and which survived until Laurie's childhood but disappeared with the decay of traditional village life. In this connection the student should consider carefully the four paragraphs that separate the suicide of Miss Flynn from the death of Mr Davies. See also p.18.

crib In the game of cribbage the cards thrown out from each player's hand are given to the dealer and are known as 'crib'.

pre-Raphaelite As in note p.36.

wind-harp i.e. Aeolian harp, a box containing strings which produce musical sounds when played on by the wind.

Morgan Perhaps the name of her own (illegitimate) child or that of an old lover. Lee has made the following comment on this reference: 'I don't think we were meant to understand Miss Flynn's reference to "Morgan". She was obviously talking to herself at that instant, about someone our faces recalled from her past.'

Home-and-Colonial The name of a widespread chain of grocery stores.

antic A complex word which seems to be used here with its earlier sense of 'old and strange'.

The Old Bugger i.e. death.

Redcoats British soldiers. Formerly red was the colour of the uniform of all regular infantry regiments.

ammonia A malapropism for 'pneumonia'.

doings i.e. private parts.

Chapter 7: Mother

Laurie's Mother was a bright and dreamy child. Much to her schoolmaster's disappointment, she had to leave school at thirteen, because of her mother's illness, to bring up her five brothers. Later, at the age of seventeen, she went into domestic service in several large houses and Laurie recounts her memories of Gaviston Court and Aldershot. When her father took a public house at Sheepscombe she went back to help him. At the age of thirty she became housekeeper to a widower in Stroud with five children, fell in love with him and married him; but, though he deserted her a few years later, she treasured her memories of married happiness for the rest of her life. Laurie describes her disorderly housekeeping, her passion for newspaper competitions and for recommending manufacturers' products. We learn of her indestructible gaiety and her unpredictable emotions, her trick of making up tart verses about local characters, her unpunctuality and her sensibility. She was an obsessive hoarder and a collector of old china, with a great love for flowers, which she grew with surprising success, and on summer nights she would play the piano. One of her romantic memories was the story of the blacksmith and the toffee-making spinster. During her last years her idiosyncracies increased and she died not long after she received the news of the death of her husband.

Commentary

It is entirely fitting that Laurie's Mother should occupy the central chapter of the book in the same way that she occupied the centre of young Laurie's life. Of all the extended portraits in *Cider with Rosie* this must surely have been the one that presented the greatest challenge in the writing. It is, of course, the most successful of all, at once loving and critical, a masterpiece of carefully accumulated detail and a wonderful tribute, which reveals in many ways how much its author owed to the woman from whom he derived directly so many of his own talents and so much of his own outlook on life – 'an interpretation of man and the natural world so unpretentious and easy that we never recognized it then, yet so true that we never forgot it.' 'I absorbed from birth,' he says, 'the whole earth through her jaunty spirit.'

From this chapter we also learn a few more details of Laurie's father, to add to the few we can glean from Chapters 1 and 4.

Quedgeley A small village about three miles south of Gloucester.
Berkeley See note p.34.
the Castle Berkeley has a splendid castle dating from the 12th century and which has been continuously inhabited since then. Here Edward II was brutally murdered in 1327.
slap-dashing Performing in a careless and hasty manner.
violet cakes Small cakes decorated with sugared violet-petals.
caste-system Society in India was divided up into hereditary classes. The members of each caste generally followed the same occupation or profession, shared the same religious rites, and had no dealings with members of another caste. In 1947 the government of India introduced regulations aimed at ending the caste system but, except amongst urban populations, these have not yet proved very effective.
myrtles In Greek mythology the myrtle was a plant sacred to Aphrodite and used as an emblem of love.
Farnhamsurrey She runs the two words together. In those days the place would seem so distant from Gloucestershire that even its name acquired an exotic and strange sound.
Aldershot This important military centre is two miles north of Farnham.
Churchdown A village four miles west of Gloucester.
Sheepscombe A small village in the next valley to Slad, about four miles out of Stroud on the road to Birdlip and Cheltenham.
the staggers The inability to walk steadily (through intoxication).
frog-march A method of carrying a drunken man or a troublesome prisoner. He is held face downward by four men, who each holds one of his limbs.

Shaw Bernard Shaw (1856–1950) wrote novels, criticism and miscellaneous journalism but is best known as a dramatist. He wrote more than twenty plays, many of them highly intellectual and satirical attacks on different aspects of modern society. Among the best known are *Pygmalion*, *Man and Superman* and *Saint Joan*. The reference to marriage occurs in 'Maxims for Revolutionaries', a kind of appendix to *Man and Superman* (1903).

Nance A familiar diminutive for 'Anne'.

jarl A dialect word, meaning to complain.

Tonks Henry Tonks (1862–1937) was an influential art teacher at the Slade School in London and an important voice in the art controversies of the turn of the century.

fire-dogs Andirons, utensils for supporting burning logs in a hearth.

Spode A type of English porcelain, named after its original manufacturer, Josiah Spode (1754–1827).

aigrette Ornamental head decoration consisting of a plume of feathers or a spray of gems.

Leamington Baths Leamington Spa is an inland health resort in Warwickshire. Water from the medicinal springs is made available to invalids in the Royal Pump Room and the Baths.

Sèvres An expensive type of porcelain of brilliant colour and delicate workmanship, manufactured at Sèvres in France since 1759.

Crown Derby A kind of china first made at Derby.

Dresden Another variety of fine porcelain, made at Meissen, near Dresden, Saxony, in Germany.

magic casements Cf. Keats's *Ode to a Nightingale:*

Magic casements, opening on the foam
Of perilous seas, in faery lands forlorn.

gravelled With an imperfectly finished surface.

Cheltenham The discovery of its mineral springs in the 18th century soon made Cheltenham Spa in Gloucestershire a fashionable town. It is about twelve miles from Slad.

hellebore A plant whose root possesses drastic purgative properties. The Christmas rose is one of the same genus.

Ern . . . nern i.e. any . . . none.

Ruskin John Ruskin (1819–1900) was probably the most influential of all 19th-century art critics and writers on aesthetics; he also wrote controversial books on economics and sociology.

Morden A suburb of Greater London, south of the river Thames.

four-year-old-daughter i.e. Frances. See the second section of Chapter 9.

Chapter 8: Winter and Summer

Childhood was dominated by winter and summer.

In winter, the light and sounds of early morning, breakfast in the kitchen – all were different; and out of doors the village boys explored a new world, helped to feed Farmer Wells's calves and went sliding and skating on Jones's pond until tea-time. The week before Christmas, when the snow lay thick, they went out at night carol singing – a five-mile journey that started at the Squire's house and ended on the hill at Farmer Joseph's.

The section on summer also begins with a description of early-morning sunlight and quickly moves to activities out of doors. The boys help to groom Mr Brown's horse; they move through a village in the grip of heat and silence to Jones's pond and the Robinsons' cottage, where they duck the pigeons in the water-butt and play cricket with the Robinson boys; and on summer nights they play games of pursuit and capture the length of the moonlit valley.

Commentary

The above summary brings out the symmetrical plan on which this chapter is constructed. Almost every aspect of winter has its summer counterpart – the 'green polar glow' of an early morning in winter, for example, is balanced by the 'pool of expanding sunlight' in summer; the feeding of Farmer Wells's calves is balanced by the grooming of Mr Brown's horse; the carol singers' five-mile tour of the area parallels the boys' hunting games over a five-mile area in summer. (See also p.14).

Each section is full of characteristic sounds and smells. The reader who makes a list of them will be surprised by their number.

dressed in dung Note the forceful overstatement.
Mercury In classical mythology he is the messenger of the gods, usually represented wearing a winged hat and winged sandals.
ice Lee is particularly fascinated by a frozen river or pond. Cf. his poem, *Boy in Ice*.
Maypole The name of a large chain of grocery stores.
tithe Lee uses the word in the sense of a source of income. Strictly, a tithe (tenth) is a contribution of one tenth of income or produce of agriculture as a due or payment to the church.
perks i.e. perquisites, legitimate profits from a position or function which are additional to a wage or salary.
King Wenslush i.e. 'Good King Wenceslas'. See note on 'O come, O come . . .', p.35.
Wild Shepherds i.e. 'While shepherds (watched their flocks by night)'.

The words of this carol are by a former Poet Laureate, Naham Tate (1652–1715).

other Joseph The husband of Mary, mother of Christ.

June high Another phrase reminiscent of Dylan Thomas. As in note on 'time hung golden and suspended', p.33.

sheepwash A place where sheep are washed before they are sheared.

tundras See note, p.34.

pampas Strictly, the grassy plains of South America.

steppes The treeless plains of Russia.

Revision questions on Chapters 5–8

1 Describe the house in which Laurie was brought up.

2 How did Granny Trill spend her time?

3 In your own words, write an account of the murder of the villager who returned from New Zealand.

4 Write a character sketch of Miss Flynn.

5 Briefly tell the story of Joseph and Hannah Brown.

6 Give an account of the early life of Laurie's Mother before she married.

7 Describe the difficulties and pleasures in the life of Laurie's Mother.

8 Write an account of the outdoor activities of Laurie and his friends *(a)* in winter, and *(b)* in summer.

Chapter 9: Sick Boy

Laurie was a sick child from birth, a fact which necessitated a hurried christening; but somehow he survived through a whole succession of ailments (watched by his youngest, short-lived sister Frances) and even being laid out as dead. Much of this chapter is devoted to the feverish nightmares of sickness. The delusion of kingship returns, the secret dream already described in Chapter 3 ('Village School') and Chapter 5 ('Grannies in the Wainscot'). By night he was often raving and delirious, and on one particular occasion he realized, for the first time, that it was possible that he might die. He confesses to enjoying the indulgence of convalescence and marvels at his subsequent heightened sensuous awareness of everything around him. Young

Laurie finally suffers concussion of the brain when he is knocked down by a cyclist.

Commentary

This chapter, more than any other, provides a showcase for Lee's handling of language. While his individual style, using imaginative language to convey subjective impressions, is of course particularly appropriate here, it might nevertheless be argued that the five long paragraphs which deal with his bouts of delirium are perhaps as feverish as their subject-matter and just a little over-wrought. Like Jack, we may wonder if he 'needed to groan quite so much'.

Adam i.e. unregenerate human nature, human sinfulness. In the Book of Common Prayer, the Order of Baptism includes the sentence: 'O merciful God, grant that the old Adam in this child may be so buried that the new man may be raised up in him.'

three names The reference books do not reveal the other two!

Cheshire-cat smiles Among the odd characters whom Alice met when she followed the White Rabbit (in Lewis Carroll's *Alice's Adventures in Wonderland*) was the Cheshire Cat, which sat on the branch of a tree and grinned and had a habit of vanishing, 'beginning with the end of the tail and ending with the grin, which remained some time after the rest of it had gone'.

Thermogene The proprietary name of a kind of dry poultice for the treatment of backache, chest pains, etc.

milk of paradise A phrase from Coleridge's poem, *Kubla Khan*.

pantheist Pantheism is the philosophical doctrine that God exists, not as a being separate from the material universe and beyond the sphere of physical experience, but in and through the physical world and nature; that God *is* the universe and everything is God.

wobbles Pain or looseness of the bowels; often referred to colloquially as 'collywobbles' (the word is a combination of *colic* and *wobble*).

bends Paralysis or pain in the joints.

Chapter 10: The Uncles

We are told little of George, Laurie's father's brother, and less of Fred. The chapter deals fully with his Mother's other four brothers, all of them skilled with horses and all of them cavalrymen in World War I.

Charlie fought in the Boer War, spent several subsequent years in South Africa and survived the massacres of Mons and Ypres before returning to Gloucestershire and becoming one of the best foresters in the Cotswolds.

Tom, a refined dandy, was pursued by women (most ardently by Effie Mansell), took a job as a tram-conductor in Worcester, eventually married Minnie and settled down as a coachman-gardener.

Ray suddenly turned up from railway camps in Canada. His main interests were drink and girls. Soon after his return to Canada he was injured and subsequently 'repaired' by a school-teacher, who married him and brought him home.

Sid, like Charlie, fought in the Boer War. He was a talented cricketer and a heroic bus-driver, whose love of drink led to his continually being suspended and various attempts at suicide. Jack and Laurie brought him home after his last attempt and he took a job as a gardener.

Commentary

Laurie's uncles, figures of legend and 'kings of our youth', throw much light for him on the way of life of the generation before his own and of those members of it who spent part of their lives away from the Cotswold valleys. They provide Lee with a fund of varied anecdotes and an opportunity for four more humorous portraits.

There is further information about Charlie and his family in Chapter 11, where we are given an account of a day's outing to Sheepscombe.

Boers Inhabitants of South Africa who are of Dutch descent. After Britain had occupied the Cape during the Napoleonic wars many of the original Dutch settlers founded the independent Boer republics of the Transvaal and the Orange Free State. Worsening relations between Britain and these two states were aggravated by the influx of British prospectors on the discovery of gold and diamonds in the Witwatersrand (or Rand) – an area of the Transvaal, the centre of which is the city of Johannesburg – and led in 1899 to the outbreak of war between Britain and the Boer states. After their initial successes the Boers were eventually defeated and President Kruger of the Transvaal, the capital of which was Pretoria, sued for peace. There was continued guerilla resistance from some groups of Boers but the war ended when a treaty was signed in 1902.

Mons, Ypres These two towns in Belgium, together with the surrounding areas near the frontier with France, were the scene of some of the most serious and costly battles of World War I.

Brassoed As in note p.33.

Flanders East and West Flanders, two provinces of Belgium lying between Brussels and the North Sea and known for centuries as 'the cockpit of Europe', were areas where some of the fiercest and most prolonged battles of World War I were fought. At Ypres there were three massive battles in 1914, 1915 and 1917.

Grimm Two brothers, Jacob (1785–1863) and William Grimm (1786–1859), both German philologists, collaborated in collecting fairy tales that had been handed down by word of mouth for generations. These they published in two volumes between 1812 and 1815.

gin-traps Metal traps for catching animals. (The word *gin* itself – a form of 'engine' – means 'trap'.)

stews Brothels.

Horsley. Sheepscombe. Rendcombe. Colne. Woodchester These are all the names of villages within a radius of ten miles from Stroud.

last year *Cider with Rosie* was first published in 1959.

Cruikshank George Cruikshank (1792–1878), one of our greatest political caricaturists, was also a great book illustrator. He provided the original illustrations for books by Scott, Dickens and Thackeray and for the first English translation of Grimms' *Fairy Tales*. The human figures in his illustrations are often comic and grotesque.

King Edward i.e. Edward VII, who reigned from 1901 to 1910.

Caliban An inhuman creature, the son of a witch, Caliban is a character in Shakespeare's *The Tempest*. He is the slave of the magician, Prospero, who punishes him by visiting upon him aches and pains.

For this, be sure, tonight thou shalt have cramps,
Side-stitches that shall pen thy breath up . . .
        . . . Thou shalt be pinched
As thick as honeycomb, each pinch more stinging
Than bees that made them (I,2, 325–9).

well-set-up This suggests that Uncle Ray had paid sums of money to the girls in order to extricate himself from promises of marriage (or even unwanted pregnancies).

Rockies The Rocky Mountains is a general name for a whole system of mountains extending down the western half of the North American continent. The highest peaks of the Canadian Rocky Mountains are over 12,000 feet high.

leviathans i.e. enormous vehicles. Originally the name of a huge sea-monster, 'leviathan' is now used to mean anything enormous.

Clevedon A small holiday town on the Severn estuary, twelve miles from Bristol.

Gothic image Medieval statue.

Chapter 11: Outings and Festivals

Village festivals revolved around the Squire – an example was the Peace Day celebration in 1919, when everyone put on fancy dress. Outings were of various kinds – family excursions to pick nuts and fruit in the remoter parts of the valley or visits to relations, like Uncle Charlie's family at Sheepscombe; and Choir Outings, like the one to Weston-super-Mare. The chapter ends with an account of the Parochial Church Tea and Annual Entertainment: the sisters' rehearsals in the kitchen, the making ready of the school, the tea itself, and then the Entertainment with contributions from Laurie (who played violin and piano duets with Eileen Brown), Mr Crosby, Major Doveton, Mrs Pimburg and Baroness von Hodenburg.

Commentary

A striking feature of this chapter is the way in which the accounts of the different occasions are presented with a considerable variety of tempo. The public bustle of the Peace Day celebration, the Choir Outing and the Parochial Church Tea and Annual Entertainment is a great contrast to the private family visit to Uncle Charlie's family. Even within the account of the latter there is great variety of pace. The children's activities in the central section are set between descriptions of the leisurely walks to and from Sheepscombe. The increasing heat and the sounds of a working morning are balanced by the darkness and the night odours on their return. Here the emphasis is on contrasting lights in the darkness – glow-worms, stars and Painswick, 'a starfish of light dilating in a pool of distance'.

moot tree In Anglo-Saxon times 'moots', official meetings of groups of citizens and counsellors, were an important feature of legal and social organization. 'Moot tree' suggests a traditional meeting place and therefore a focal point in the life of the village.

John Bull The traditional personification of England, usually portrayed wearing a frock-coat, white breeches, high boots, a top-hat and a union-jack waistcoat, and accompanied by a bulldog.

we wasn't The incorrect grammar, besides making the account more realistic, suggests the anti-climax of this formal speech.

Peter the Pieman Note the alliteration in the names of this and the previous reference. Lee writes: 'Peter the Pieman was a figure from our youth. He wore baker's white, carried a basket of pies for sale round the streets and rang a bell. Perhaps his fame was only local.'

a group by the rockery This photograph is one of many which are reproduced in *The Illustrated Cider with Rosie* (Century Publishing Co.).

Scrubs As in note p.40.

Gramp i.e. grandpa.

earth closet Outdoor privy.

'I remember . . .' The best known poem of Thomas Hood (1798–1845), editor and writer of humorous verse and poems of more serious social comment, like the *Song of the Shirt*.

horse-brake A large open wagonette with four wheels.

charabanc Early name for a motor coach.

Bristol Far from being at the ends of the earth, Bristol is about thirty miles from Slad. Weston-super-Mare, on the Severn estuary, is twenty miles farther.

Woolpack The name of the village inn.

Clifton Gorges At Clifton, on the outskirts of Bristol, the river Avon flows through an impressive gorge.

nightmares The peepshows on the pier – lighted boxes into which one looked through lenses at mechanically moving models of lurid happenings.

Newgate The most notorious of all the old London prisons. It was used from the 12th century until 1880.

cataleptic Catalepsy is a condition of nervous disorder in which the patient's limbs, as if in a trance or seizure, remain fixed in any positon in which they are placed.

Twelfth Night The traditional festivities and merrymaking of Christmas lasted for twelve days. The Twelfth Night after Christmas is January 5th, the eve of the Feast of the Epiphany.

fly-cake Children's name for a cake containing currants.

Mother Hawkins . . . geese Children's way of saying 'It is snowing'. In some parts of the country it is simply 'The old woman is plucking her geese.'

Urdu Major Doveton would have spoken Urdu in India. It is Hindustani as used generally among Mohammedans and is a language understood and used as a means of communication all over India.

sink i.e. sing.

convected i.e. concocted, composed.

Bose vords und i.e. both words and.

Chapter 12: First Bite at the Apple

A description of early sexual explorations with the silent and complaisant Jo leads to a discussion of village morality and of crime and punishment. At the age of puberty the girls come into their own and we are introduced to brazen Bet and provocative Rosie Burdock, with whom Laurie spends an afternoon and evening, kissing and drinking cider underneath a hay-wagon. They share an intense physical and emotional experience and when they return home at night Laurie feels like a giant and raised to a higher level of existence. Later half a dozen of the boys plan the rape of Lizzy Berkeley in Brith Wood but their innate sense of shame in the end defeats their desires.

Commentary

Apart from the story that Lee tells, this chapter is notable for containing a greater ration of *ideas* than any other chapter except the final one. The village community's attitude to, and methods of dealing with, social and sexual transgressions are discussed in detail and approved of.

The description of the sensations and emotions of puberty is a beautifully written paragraph and leads naturally to the episode in the hayfield, when Rosie Burdock decides to extend Laurie's sexual experience. What might, in the hands of another writer, have turned out to be a titillating and tasteless account, is told with tact, in prose which has the richness and rhythms of poetry.

The sexual urges of adolescents, 'confused by our strength and boredom', also lie behind the planning of the Brith Wood rape. This episode too is recounted with restraint, understanding and, at the end, a certain amount of irony.

first bite at the apple i.e. the beginnings of sexual knowledge.
Battersea boys i.e. boys brought up in cities and large towns. Battersea is part of the London borough of Wandsworth.
tricky wood i.e. adolescent uncertainty amid the problems of sex.
banks . . . tiring-houses In Shakespeare's *A Midsummer Night's Dream* a group of workmen hold rehearsals for a play in the wood outside Athens. One of them, Bottom the weaver, says:

Here's a marvellous convenient place for our rehearsal. This green plot shall be our stage, this hawthorn-brake our tiring-house.

In an Elizabethan theatre a tiring-house was a dressing-room. (In Lee's context the word implies rather an *un*dressing-room!)
Gis i.e. give us.
green-horned Lacking in experience.
possles i.e. apostles.
It'll half be . . . i.e. it won't half be . . . See note on 'You're 'alf . . .', p.37.

Chapter 13: Last Days

The end of Laurie's childhood coincides with the end of traditional village life, as motor-cars and buses, picture-palaces and wireless aerials link the village directly with the world outside and the rhythms and values of the village are swamped in the tide of noise and speed. The church retains for a time its spiritual hold; the pattern of Sunday continues – burnt sausages for breakfast, the learning of the Collect, Sunday School, morning service and evensong – and the cycle of the church year remains, with Harvest Festival making a special impression. On the death of the Squire the estate is broken up; with the coming of 'fragmentation, free thought and new excitements' the hold of the church weakens; and as the old people die the links with the past are broken. The last days of the family also draw near – the sisters are courted by young men (Marjorie by Maurice the barge-builder, Dorothy by Leslie the scoutmaster, Phyllis by Harold the bootmaker), and brother Harold brings home a girl. There is a disorderly picnic and engagements bring high feelings and family quarrels. It is a time of change for Laurie too: adolescence brings solitary wanderings, with a sense of destiny and the raging excitement of love, expressed in poem after poem.

Commentary

It seems fitting that our last meeting with Laurie's family, on the occasion of the quarrel over a fiancé, should be in the kitchen, the setting for so much earlier activity, 'the common room we shared'.

The second paragraph of this chapter explains, with particular force for the younger student, the importance of the horse, for both power and transport, before the coming of the internal combustion engine (p.216).

For a time the village community observed the protocol of class differences and the order of seating in church reflected the social hierarchy which had been acknowledged for centuries.

The structure of this chapter is carefully planned so that changes in the external and material aspects of village life and in people's ways of thinking are mirrored by the changes in Laurie's family, where 'new manners and new notions crept in', and finally in Laurie himself.

wagonette An open horse-drawn carriage with four wheels and facing seats along the sides.

lion . . . lamb The reference embodies a fairly common misquotation from Isaiah, 11,6:

The wolf also shall dwell with the lamb, and the leopard shall lie down with the kid; and the calf and the young lion and the fatling together.

horn of plenty The cornucopia, an emblem of plenty and abundance in classical mythology. Amalthea, a daughter of the King of Crete, nursed the infant Zeus and fed him with goat's milk. As a sign of his gratitude Zeus broke off one of the goat's horns and gave it the power to produce whatever its possessor wished. It is often depicted as filled with fruits and flowers.

one foundation Cf.the hymn by S. J. Stone:

The Church's one foundation is Jesus Christ, her Lord.

'All . . . gathered in' A line from the harvest hymn, 'Come, ye thankful people, come', by H. Alford.

Sons and Lovers This great novel, published in 1913 by D. H. Lawrence (1885–1930), is largely autobiographical and deals with the conflicting relationships of a Nottingham miner's son with his mother and the women he loves. The vicar no doubt confiscated the book as much on account of Lawrence's reputation at that time as for the outspoken treatment (for those days) of its story.

apologist One who is prepared to defend his opinions by argument. In this respect the new vicar is a contrast with his authoritarian predecessor.

shoot Offshoot, descendant.

I ain't nurn a aypence i.e. I have no halfpennies.

recollect i.e. remember (or perhaps recompense).

crack-jawed Speaking unnaturally carefully and correctly.

Savoy Orpheans A popular dance band of the earliest days of broadcasting, from 1922 onwards. The first studios of the BBC were at Savoy Hill, near the Savoy Hotel, in London. 'Orpheans' means followers of Orpheus, who, in Greek legend, played the lyre so skilfully that even wild beasts and inanimate objects were moved by his music.

Revision questions on Chapters 9–13

1 What were the pleasures of Laurie's periods of convalescence?

2 Compare and contrast the lives and personalities of Uncle Tom and Uncle Ray.

3 In your own words, write an account of the Peace Day celebrations of 1919.

4 Describe either *(a)* the Choir Outing to Weston-super-Mare, or *(b)* the Parochial Church Tea and Annual Entertainment.

5 What general comments does the author make on village morality?

6 Write an account of the Brith Wood rape.

7 What does the author tell us of the courting of his sisters?

General questions

Note style answer

1 By what means does young Laurie learn about life and events in the Cotswold valley before his own time?

From his *Mother*: he learns how she helped her father when he was landlord of the Plough Inn – handling drunkards and accommodating the few remaining carters. Her story of the blacksmith and the toffee-making spinster.

From *Granny Trill*: her life in a tent in the woods with her father, a woodcutter; she made baskets, which she sold to villagers. After her father's death she was looked after by the Squire.

From *Uncle Charlie*: the life of a forester – his skill and the extent of his work; bringing up a family on thirty-five shillings a week.

From *traditional village lore*: the tragedy of the Bulls Cross hangman; stories of violence and death (fights, suicides, people killed by animals).

2 Write a description, as detailed as possible, of the house in which Laurie Lee's family and the two old ladies lived.

3 On a large sheet of paper draw a diagram in the form of a family tree containing all the author's family and relations who are mentioned in *Cider with Rosie*. Wherever you can, enter their approximate dates of birth and death. (Including the wives of Laurie's uncles, your diagram should contain twenty-three characters).

4 Show how the lives of Granny Trill and Granny Wallon 'revolved in intimate enmity around each other'.

5 What do we learn from *Cider with Rosie* of Laurie's father?

6 The most detailed of all the personal portraits in *Cider with Rosie* is that of Laurie's Mother. What, in your opinion, are her most important or striking qualities?

7 Which of Laurie's uncles appeals to you most, and why?

8 What do you know of the six Robinson children?

9 Write character sketches of Laurie's three half-sisters and show how they differed from one another.

10 Write about Laurie's childhood illnesses. How does he describe his feelings when he was ill and when he was recovering?

11 How did Laurie's early schooling differ from your own? Do you think he had any advantages which you did not have?

12 What impact did World War I have upon the childhood of Laurie Lee?

13 Do you think Lee is better at describing young people or old people? Support your answer by referring in some detail to at least three characters.

14 Which of Lee's characters seems to you the most unusual or eccentric? Describe the person you have chosen so as to bring out fully his or her unusual characteristics.

15 Of all the villagers described in *Cider with Rosie* which would you most like to have as a neighbour? Explain why.

16 'Perhaps there are too many people in *Cider with Rosie*.' What do *you* think? Give reasons for your answer.

17 'The last days of my childhood were also the last days of the village.' Explain this sentence, illustrating your explanation with direct reference to *Cider with Rosie*.

18 'The sun and moon, which once rose from our hill, rose from London now in the east.' Show how the arrival of new values and ideas began to change the villagers' traditional pattern of life.

19 What does Lee say about crime and punishment and about the villagers' attitudes towards them? Are these attitudes different from your own?

20 'Time and the changes which time brings, to the individual and to the community, are the main themes of *Cider with Rosie*.' Discuss this statement, with close reference to the book.

21 'There, with a sense of bewilderment and terror, my life in the village began.' By means of reference and quotation show the part which bewilderment and terror occupy in *Cider with Rosie*.

22 By means of quotation and close reference illustrate some of the characteristic ways in which Lee handles words.

23 What does Lee mean by 'the stain of darkness upon my brow' (Chapter 9)? What evidence of it do you find in *Cider with Rosie*?

24 In reading *Cider with Rosie* what has appealed to you most? Which parts of the book have had least appeal to you? In both cases, give your reasons.

25 Imagine you have been asked to supply for a local historical society a purely factual description of the village of Slad as it was from about 1910 to about 1920. Write your account, using what you have learned from *Cider with Rosie*.

26 Lee gives us minor histories of several characters with whom he and his family have little direct connection (e.g. Miss Flynn, Squire Jones, Vincent from New Zealand, Mr and Mrs Davies, Joseph and Hannah Brown). Write an account of some of these characters whom you have found particularly interesting.

27 Select one of your favourite chapters. While re-reading it, write down some of the most striking sentences and expressions and try to explain why you find them effective.

28 'I remember very clearly how it started. It was summer, and we boys were sitting on the bank watching a great cloud of smoke in the sky.' What does this refer to, and why is the occasion a significant one?

Further reading

Laurie Lee: *The Illustrated Cider with Rosie*. Century Publishing Company, 1984.
As well as reproductions of country scenes painted by artists mostly working in the 1920s and 1930s, here are forty-four contemporary photographs of people and activities connected with Slad, Stroud and Painswick. Among these photographs are sixteen from Laurie Lee's own collection which show the cottage, the family, Laurie's school class (including Laurie, Jack, the Robinson boys and Rosie Burdock), the Peace celebrations and many others.

Joan Tucker: *Stroud as it was*. Hendon Publishing Company, 1978.
This book contains more than sixty photographs, with detailed descriptive captions, showing almost every aspect of life and work in a Cotswold town in the first two decades of the present century. There are photographs of the cloth mills and shops in Stroud, where Laurie's sisters worked; of activities like pageants and civic celebrations; of fashions in dress and various forms of transport of the period; and a photograph of the Annual Slad Choir Outing.

Laurie Lee: *I Can't Stay Long*. Penguin Books, 1977.
Part One contains seven autobiographical essays, in which Lee writes of his boyhood reading and the world as he imagined it when he was eight years old. Three of the essays deal with recollections similar to those related in *Cider with Rosie*: 'Whitsuntide Treat', 'A Drink with a Witch' and 'First Love'. 'An Obstinate Exile' is about living in London. The final essay discusses the writing of autobiography and of *Cider with Rosie* in particular.

Pan study aids

W. H. Auden Selected Poetry

Jane Austen Emma Mansfield Park Northanger Abbey Persuasion
Pride and Prejudice

Anthologies of Poetry Ten Twentieth Century Poets The Poet's Tale
The Metaphysical Poets

Samuel Beckett Waiting for Godot

Arnold Bennett The Old Wives' Tale

William Blake Songs of Innocence and Experience

Robert Bolt A Man for All Seasons

Harold Brighouse Hobson's Choice

Charlotte Brontë Jane Eyre

Emily Brontë Wuthering Heights

Robert Browning Selected Poetry

John Bunyan The Pilgrim's Progress

Geoffrey Chaucer (parallel texts editions) The Franklin's Tale
The Knight's Tale The Miller's Tale The Nun's Priest's Tale
The Pardoner's Tale Prologue to the Canterbury Tales
The Wife of Bath's Tale

Richard Church Over the Bridge

John Clare Selected Poetry and Prose

Samuel Taylor Coleridge Selected Poetry and Prose

Wilkie Collins The Woman in White

William Congreve The Way of the World

Joseph Conrad The Nigger of the Narcissus & Youth
The Secret Agent

Charles Dickens Bleak House David Copperfield Dombey and Son
Great Expectations Hard Times Little Dorrit Oliver Twist
Our Mutual Friend A Tale of Two Cities

Gerald Durrell My Family and Other Animals

George Eliot Middlemarch The Mill on the Floss Silas Marner

T. S. Eliot Murder in the Cathedral Selected Poems

J. G. Farrell The Siege of Krishnapur

Henry Fielding Joseph Andrews

F. Scott Fitzgerald The Great Gatsby

E. M. Forster Howards End A Passage to India
Where Angels Fear to Tread

William Golding Lord of the Flies The Spire

Oliver Goldsmith Two Plays of Goldsmith: She Stoops to Conquer;
The Good Natured Man

Graham Greene Brighton Rock The Power and the Glory
The Quiet American

Thom Gunn and Ted Hughes Selected Poems

Thomas Hardy Chosen Poems of Thomas Hardy
Far from the Madding Crowd Jude the Obscure
The Mayor of Casterbridge Return of the Native
Tess of the d'Urbervilles The Trumpet-Major

L. P. Hartley The Go-Between The Shrimp and the Anemone

Joseph Heller Catch-22

Ernest Hemingway For Whom the Bell Tolls
The Old Man and the Sea

Barry Hines A Kestrel for a Knave

Gerard Manley Hopkins Poetry and Prose of Gerard Manley Hopkins

Aldous Huxley Brave New World

Henry James Washington Square

Ben Jonson The Alchemist Volpone

James Joyce Dubliners A Portrait of the Artist as a Young Man

John Keats Selected Poems and Letters of John Keats

Ken Kesey One Flew over the Cuckoo's Nest

Rudyard Kipling Kim

D. H. Lawrence The Rainbow Selected Tales Sons and Lovers

Harper Lee To Kill a Mockingbird

Laurie Lee As I Walked out One Midsummer Morning
Cider with Rosie

Thomas Mann Death in Venice & Tonio Kröger

Christopher Marlowe Doctor Faustus Edward the Second

W. Somerset Maugham Of Human Bondage

Gavin Maxwell Ring of Bright Water

Thomas Middleton and William Rowley The Changeling

Arthur Miller The Crucible Death of a Salesman

John Milton A Choice of Milton's Verse Comus and Samson
Agonistes Paradise Lost I, II

Sean O'Casey Juno and the Paycock
The Shadow of a Gunman and the Plough and the Stars

George Orwell Animal Farm 1984

John Osborne Luther

Alexander Pope Selected Poetry

J. B. Priestley An Inspector Calls

Siegfried Sassoon Memoirs of a Fox-Hunting Man

Peter Shaffer The Royal Hunt of the Sun

William Shakespeare Antony and Cleopatra As You Like It
Coriolanus Hamlet Henry IV (Part I) Henry IV (Part II) Henry V
Julius Caesar King Lear Love's Labour's Lost Macbeth Measure for
Measure The Merchant of Venice A Midsummer Night's Dream
Much Ado about Nothing Othello Richard II Richard III Romeo and
Juliet The Sonnets The Taming of the Shrew The Tempest Twelfth
Night The Winter's Tale

G. B. Shaw Androcles and the Lion Arms and the Man
Caesar and Cleopatra The Doctor's Dilemma Pygmalion Saint Joan

Richard Sheridan Plays of Sheridan: The Rivals; The Critic;
The School for Scandal

John Steinbeck The Grapes of Wrath Of Mice and Men & The Pearl

Tom Stoppard Rosencrantz and Guildenstern are Dead

J. M. Synge The Playboy of the Western World

Jonathan Swift Gulliver's Travels

Alfred Tennyson Selected Poetry

William Thackeray Vanity Fair

Flora Thompson Lark Rise to Candleford

Dylan Thomas Under Milk Wood

Anthony Trollope Barchester Towers

Mark Twain Huckleberry Finn

Keith Waterhouse Billy Liar

Evelyn Waugh Decline and Fall Scoop

H. G. Wells The History of Mr Polly The War of the Worlds

John Webster The Duchess of Malfi The White Devil

Oscar Wilde The Importance of Being Earnest

Virginia Woolf To the Lighthouse

William Wordsworth The Prelude (Books 1, 2)

William Wycherley The Country Wife

John Wyndham The Chrysalids

W. B. Yeats Selected Poetry

Pan study aids

Published jointly by Heinemann Educational Books and Pan Books

Pan Study Aids is a major new series developed to help school and college students prepare for examinations. All the authors are experienced teachers/examiners at O level, School Certificate and equivalent examinations and authors of textbooks used in schools and colleges worldwide

Each volume in the series:
- explains its subject and covers clearly and concisely and with excellent illustrations the essential points of the syllabus, drawing attention to common areas of difficulty and to areas which carry most marks in the exam

- gives guidance on how to plan revision, and prepare for the exam, outlining what examiners are looking for

- provides practice by including typical exam questions and exercises

Titles available: Physics, Chemistry, Maths, Human Biology, English Language, Geography 1 & 2, Economics, Commerce, Accounts and Book-keeping, British Government and Politics, History 1 & 2, Effective Study Skills, French, German, Spanish, Sociology